First Facts™

Our Government

The City Council

by Terri DeGezelle

Consultant:
Michael Reinemer
Director of Communications
The National League of Cities
Washington, D.C.

Capstone press

Mankato, Minnesota

First Facts is published by Capstone Press,
151 Good Counsel Drive, P.O. Box 669, Mankato, Minnesota 56002.
www.capstonepress.com

Library of Congress Cataloging-in-Publication Data
DeGezelle, Terri, 1955–
    The city council / by Terri DeGezelle.
        p. cm.—(First facts. Our government)
    Includes bibliographical references and index.
    ISBN 0-7368-3684-5 (hardcover)
    1. Municipal government—United States—Juvenile literature. 2. City councils—United
States—Juvenile literature. I. Title. II. Series.
JS346.D44 2005
320.8'54—dc22   2004010938

Summary: Describes city government, including how city councils are elected and pass
    new ordinances.

Editorial Credits
Christine Peterson, editor; Jennifer Bergstrom, set designer; Enoch Peterson, book designer;
    Jo Miller, photo researcher

Photo Credits
All photographs by Gregg Andersen/Gallery 19 except page 20, Capstone Press/Karon Dubke

1 2 3 4 5 6 10 09 08 07 06 05

Table of Contents

City Councils Serve Cities

In the United States, city councils are part of city governments. People elect council members to serve their city. City councils listen to the needs of **citizens**. Council members pass new laws, such as laws about garbage and water. They work to improve their city.

Most city governments have three parts. **Mayors** lead most cities. Councils make new city laws. Local courts decide what laws mean.

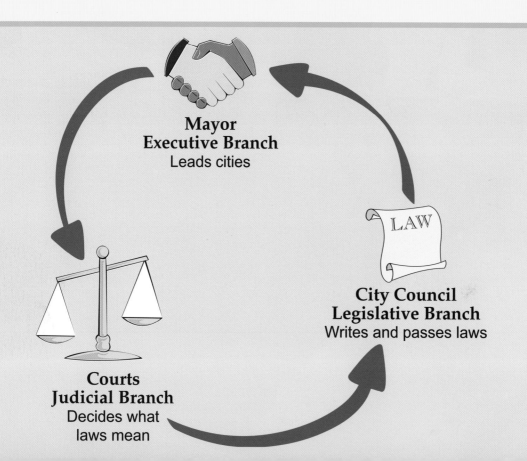

Mayor
Executive Branch
Leads cities

City Council
Legislative Branch
Writes and passes laws

Courts
Judicial Branch
Decides what laws mean

Councils write and pass new city
laws called **ordinances**. They make laws
about streets, pets, noise, and buildings.
Councils oversee city **services**.

Council Members

Most city councils have five to nine members. At least 20 people serve on councils in large cities. Most council members serve for one, two, or four years. In most cities, council members must be at least 18 years old.

Fact!
New York City has 51 city council members.

9

Cities Have Wards

Cities are divided into parts called **wards**. One person from each ward serves on the city council. Citizens of a ward talk to their council members about planned laws and other **issues**. Council members work to help people in their wards.

Councils Meet with People

City councils listen to ideas from people in the community. They meet with business owners. They talk about laws and jobs.

Council members also talk about city services. They meet with police officers. They discuss ways to keep people safe.

RUTH KAGERMEIER
Mayor

Councils Work with Mayors

City councils work with mayors to make cities better. The mayor leads the council. Council members and the mayor decide how to spend city money. They work to improve city streets, parks, and water.

Councils Have Committees

Council members and citizens serve on **committees**. They talk about issues and laws. They discuss what services the city needs.

Council members also meet in small groups. They plan laws and services. They discuss ways to raise and spend city money.

Councils Pass Laws

City councils meet to pass new city ordinances. At meetings, citizens give their thoughts about a planned law. Council members discuss the need for a law. The council then votes. If the idea passes, the mayor signs it into law.

Fact!
In some cities, mayors only vote when there is a tie.

18

Amazing but True!

City councils sometimes pass the strangest laws. In Lexington, New Jersey, it's against the law to carry an ice cream cone in your pocket. Watch out for weeds in Pueblo, Colorado. In that city, it's against the law to let dandelions grow. In Columbus, Ohio, it is against the law to sell cornflakes on Sunday.

Hands On: Write Your Council

Write a letter to a member of your city council. Invite your city council member to visit your school and help your class learn more about city government.

What You Need

paper	postage stamp
pen or pencil	an adult to help
envelope	

What You Do

1. Find the address for your city council member in your local newspaper. Addresses can also be found at local libraries and on your city's Internet site.
2. Begin your letter with "Dear Council Member:"
3. Ask your council member what projects or laws he or she is working on for the city.
4. Invite your council member to visit your school.
5. Sign your letter and place it in an envelope.
6. Address the envelope and place a postage stamp on the upper right hand corner.
7. Ask an adult to help you mail the letter.

Glossary

citizen (SIT-i-zuhn)—a member of a country, state, or city who has the right to live there

committee (kuh-MIT-ee)—a group of people chosen to discuss things and make decisions for a larger group

issue (ISH-oo)—an idea or need that is talked about by citizens and government leaders

mayor (MAY-ur)—the leader of a city

ordinance (OR-din-anss)—a law made by a city government

service (SUR-viss)—a system or way of providing something useful or necessary; city services include providing streets, water, and parks.

ward (WARD)—a part of a town or city

Read More

Flanagan, Alice K. *Mayors.* Community Workers. Minneapolis: Compass Point Books, 2001.

Giesecke, Ernestine. *Local Government.* Kids' Guide. Chicago: Heinemann, 2000.

Internet Sites

FactHound offers a safe, fun way to find Internet sites related to this book. All of the sites on FactHound have been researched by our staff.

Here's how:
1. Visit *www.facthound.com*
2. Type in this special code **0736836845** for age-appropriate sites. Or enter a search word related to this book for a more general search.
3. Click on the **Fetch It** button.

FactHound will fetch the best sites for you!

Index